Difficult Joy

Difficult Joy

poems by
Brian Glaser

SHANTI ARTS PUBLISHING
BRUNSWICK, MAINE

Difficult Joy

Published by Shanti Arts Publishing
Interior and cover design by Shanti Arts Designs

Shanti Arts LLC
193 Hillside Road
Brunswick, Maine 04011

shantiarts.com

Cover and interior image by Marek Piwnicki / unsplash.com

The original German version of Hölderlin's "Brod
und Wein" was taken from germanlit.org:
https://sites.google.com/site/germanliterature/19th-
century/hoelderlin/brot-und-wein-bread-and-wine

Printed in the United States of America

ISBN: 978-1-956056-14-3 (softcover)

Library of Congress Control Number: 2021948662

for Mary Ellen Glaser

Contents

Acknowledgments

Poems in this collection have appeared or will soon appear in these venues, gratefully acknowledged:

Artistic Differences Project:	"Critical Portrait"
Egophobia:	"Mind-way"
Ephemeral Elegies:	"Mission San Juan Capistrano"
Ethical ELA:	"On Surf Guitar"
Ezra:	"Bread and Wine"
Isacoustic:	"Difficult Joy: A Prelude"
Lunate:	"Santa Ana Mountains"
The Nervous Breakdown:	"On Insects"
Red River Review:	"To a Historian Perhaps Unborn"

The "One Echo" section of this book was written over the course of a faculty development leave funded by Chapman University. Special thanks to Joanna Levin and Jennifer Keene for their support.

And thanks to Brenda Hillman for the phrase that gives this book its title.

Difficult Joy

"Each dance and its music *belong* to a time and place. It can be borrowed elsewhere, or later in time, but it will never be in its moment again. When these little cultural blooms are past, they become ethnic or nostalgic, but never quite fully present—manifesting the web of their original connections and meanings—again."

—Gary Snyder, *The Practice of the Wild*

To a Historian Perhaps Unborn

The photographer Edward Cochems was born in Chicago in 1874.
In 1902, he married Emma Glaser. In 1904, their daughter was born.
Edward moved to Santa Ana in 1915. He lived here for thirty years.

1

He faces his daughter from five paces,
she gazes towards him with her hands in her lap.

He stands by the camera,
she casts a shape on a painted scene.

To photograph is to confer importance:
who would disagree?

Over one hundred unidentified subjects
are among the thousand photos that he left.

This one was taken in the year
after the outbreak of the Spanish flu.

His body—in a suit—blocks the view
of the camera on which his hand rests

and equidistant from them both
a diffusing screen reads pure, empty white.

2

He had a nervous breakdown—that is,
he was unable for a time to work

while he was supporting his family as
a salesman in Los Angeles just before the Great War.

He might have made one of Paul Strand's
pedestrians raked by morning light in a canyon of commerce

if he had put on spiritual defeat.
Instead at nearly age forty he began the work

he would later call "How I Won My Way
Back to Health with Photography."

As he wrote about the stream
that wends through the arroyo of Aliso Canyon in 1933:

Truly a wondrous spot somewhat hidden
on the unbeaten path from the eye of the tourist.

Difficult Joy • A Prelude

1

someone's a wren
tugging at the sun;

the fire's throat
on the last lectern—

added to them
just in time

—night newborn,
you will say maybe—

2

the spirit of a magnet
against the spirit

of the rain—

a number in the garden:

your second beard,
the literal meaning

of the four
memories at once—

3

what the leafless trees add
is nothing

to the tally of whiteness—

death's creek—
a broken doorbell—

4

darkroom of a deacon—

the exultant slide to the corner
of the pitch—

5

dark energy,
a mass,—

Cherry Garcia—
save me some,

I will lick it happily
from your knuckle—

Difficult Joy

1

the boy sits
on the boat—

dare to look
in the water,

lost wind,—

what you see there,

how did it grow
up from

the earth

as in
heaven's mirror
before—

2

in the water,
the red line—

not your fault
at rest

speaking
from the blue ground;

where the lover
now plays the father

who taps twice
again on the boards—

and if we were gods

the healing
would have a thought-
purse—

so let's not

pay
the absolute
price—

3

like the game—
the hearth on the table

whose heat draws your heart
in the mind's distance—

the blackness of the bird
or of the tree,

this open character—

the earth's architecture has no fear
of its emptiness,

though the architect may—

she will play
in death's distance,

heart-mind
today

is the laughter of the worm—

4

no:
not anonymous,

another's
early image:

a chorus of smiles—

circling the dorm in the autumn alone,
utterly lost

and afraid—

though absence is everywhere,

yet presence
is everywhere too—

in the cold reaches of space,
presence is—

in the autumnal sadness,
presence is—

presence is,

a chorus of smiles,
he sees them, I see them there—

so tonight

they survived
a lost man's

first walk
as the darkness—

5

the parable

of the burning house
in the lotus sutra—

the loss-light in which
the father

cannot lie,

the acid-love
of the moth's

golden wing-flame

6

the cathedral
and the river sin—

prayer
and the river stone—

like the canvas
of the green,—

we should try
to be more each day
like the patient-plant,—

tell it to the fruits—

to the seed
inside the stone,

the prayer-skin
like the leather

of the rose—

7

this five days ago—
read of it today:

a murder
in the park

where I played with my children,
three they called transients

used a knife
on his torso,

the newspaper says
he bled profusely

and life-saving measures failed,—

tomorrow we will light a candle
and read there the poem

that begins

no man is an island—

the nameless way
runs through the neighbor-night

8

the sage can be inhumane
to the masses

our quiet ceremony was,
my eldest pronounced it good—

like the elderly priest,
Christopher,

buying produce
in the time of the disease,

it is impossible to step backwards
on some stages

Early April

Thunder—
will the mountain lions find
one another there?

Santa Ana Mountains

—for my father, John Glaser

The Fire Poppy

It only flowers for a few seasons
after a wildfire
and then it disappears.

I know it exists here from books—
I have never
seen it in these mountains—
it may be found only in the shrubland close to the ocean.

Some things books are good enough for.

They are like our small mountain range
surrounded by the larger ranges
of the basin,

our mountains out of
cross-beds of sedimentary and volcanic layers of rock.

Some like the sedimentary layers
because you can find in them traces of life.

I like the idea of them—
how the ocean seems to have worked to leave a legacy for us:

the way dreaming
on land for long enough can make it yours.

Chaparral

Your friend whose father died
when he was a boy—

it was a wound because it was his fear.

A fear
that seems like a dare to you,
a dare to continue loving intensely
when you are a boy,
though you have no choice.

Say it: the enemy is the grass.

One fire, the years pass—
our burls in the earth are safe there—
call it a sanctuary.

Too many fires in too few years—
then the grasses win.

Separation—
too much separation and you learn
to speak like a grave.

South-Facing Slope

It's all relative, of course,
the sharpness of the wounds of loss.

I have less,
drought becomes my bed.

It's how memory works here,
drought.

So when you hear them say it's all ultimately one—
that's your religion, the Tao—

that's the rhetoric of the south-facing slope.
Here loss, the ridge,
hides a richer nature from you as you climb.

Sacrifice:
that's the rhetoric of the north-facing slope.

Rhetoric has its purposes.
If it cannot change very much about the world,
it can keep you from lying to yourself—

dark green,
the tenacious tense of the past:

these were your mountains,
you who loved and were loved.

On Insects

1

During the quarantine, we were all in the living room,
the four of us, playing a game,
an unremarkable afternoon in April,
National Poetry Month,
and a small bird flew in through the dog's foot-wide opening
in the sliding glass door to the backyard,
and the dog, Berkeley,
sprang up and barked and ran to the dining room
where the bird was fluttering against the glass and falling—
I could hear it, it was painful—
and before we could protest enough he had killed the small
gray-feathered bird with a swift, vicious bite.

2

I am a connoisseur of melancholia
with depression everywhere in my family on my mother's side
and so, after years of therapy,
I am suspicious of, even resentful of,
those who are attracted to the sadness of the suffering of others
because, as I see things, it helps them make sense of, or,
worse, feel virtuous about, their own woundedness.
I thought of this as I found the bird on the linoleum,
breathing with the last, sad, harried energy of the dying,
and I felt a wave of grief
and then a hatred—sorry for the necessary word—hatred of that grief,
and then—familiar—the lightness of an idea of the poem,
and then—this is new, in my accession to middle age—
just simple grief again,
awareness of the dying sunlit room in which I stood, its historicity.

3

Our house is built over a concrete slab
that was poured on the lot after an orange orchard was axed
in the sixties to build our neighborhood,
mostly nondescript modern houses, with two stately Victorians
owned by real estate agents
and kept in perfect performance of repair.
Shortly after we moved in a horde of termites appeared
under the kitchen window in the back yard
and the exterminator I called in told me that every nine years or so
the colony of termites that lives on the dead roots of the orchard
in the absolute darkness
under the slab
shoots up into daylight—
he seemed delighted as he told me all this
with a salesman's unfeigned appreciative energy
that I know from my mother's side of the family as well,
amoral and indefatigable.

4

Issa is the haiku poet of insects.
They will probably always have their day before and more often than
the losers of the wars of human history,
and there are so many of them in the spring and summer here,
the crickets,
that I cannot locate them in the yard
and so it can seem to me that at least some of them are inside the house
until I close the glass door
and I hear them as what Wallace Stevens called
the minor of what we feel.
Minor:
the insect's sound in contrast with the song of the bird,
one rasping note,
on or off,
half-nothing—the difference between mercy and grace.

On Surf Guitar

1

It was the first contribution of this seat, Orange County,
to world music—
after the heyday of the KKK here, in the depths of segregation
of our neighborhoods—
at a nightspot on the island of Balboa in the early sixties
Dick Dale played Lebanese melodic lines
on the novel electric guitar
backed by a battery of rapid drums and a modest bass
and, yes, for a season, for a couple of years,
the world took note,
there was, as Gertrude Stein said in *Tender Buttons*,
no use in a center.

2

My eldest has a playlist
of surf guitar on his phone—still a genre, long after the Beach Boys
alloyed it with vocal harmonies
and the Beatles swept its influence away like a wall of water
and nostalgic movies
rediscovered it and fused it to an image,
a star's charisma,
and my son has worn his index finger to a blister
playing surf guitar in his room,
and has worried aloud about whether to stop for a while and heal
or to keep playing so the blister
gives painfully way to the callus you really need for his art.

3

It is arbitrary, the relation between Dale's music
and the practice of surfing—
it's untrue that the reverb means the sound of the breaking waves—
arbitrary, but by time connected here, so that to some,
like me,
surfing itself can seem like a nostalgic art,
the fit, bobbing acolytes of the rhythms of the ocean living out
a new postwar discovery
like the improvisatory scores of the Judson Church dancers,
from the same era,
when art and life seemed in America to be two sides of a glass,
as artists have so long wanted them to be,
which is why we work so hard at our art—
I think second nature's secret promise
has always been
to be more human than this, our blood-freaked first.

und wozu Dichter in dürftiger Zeit?

—Friedrich Hölderlin

Bread and Wine

—for Brenda Hillman, from Hölderlin's "Brod und Wein"

1

The sleeping city surrounds us; the lit streets are falling quiet
   And the coaches rush away, adorned with torches' fire.
People are headed home, contented by the good in their days
   And cheered by the reckoning that sets their profits against their losses,
The well-weighted scales. No more grapes or flowers in the markets,
   No more handicrafts for the many who visited there today.
But string-music can be heard from distant gardens;
   A lover, perhaps, is playing, or a lonely man is practicing
And thinking of distant friends or his youth; the fountains,
   Just learning to speak, and the fragrant flowerbeds astir.
The dusk seems still as the bells ring out across the sky
   And a guardian calls out the hour he has watched approaching.
Now, too, a breeze stirs the tree-crowns in the wood,
   And—look!—the shadow-image of our Earth, the moon
Comes out in secret; wild-minded, the night comes out,
   Full of stars and not very much concerned about us,
Shining with astonishing intensity, utterly alien to humankind,
   In sadness and beauty breaking over the mountain heights.

2

The benevolence of night, the exalted, is like a miracle—
    No one knows how or when she works her transformations.
She moves the world and the hopeful souls of us humans,
    And even the wise cannot say what she is preparing—
The almighty God who loves you ordains it to be so.
    And so to you the clarity of day is more dear,
Though sometimes even clear eyes long for the shadows,
    Trying the pleasure of sleep before it calls to them,
And a good man can desire to look deeply into the night.
    So it is right to consecrate garlands and to sing of her
Because she is sacred to those lost in madness and the dead,
    She who partakes of the eternal, a free spirit for all time.
She also makes descend upon us oblivion and spiritual ecstasy,
    We who live in the trembling medium of time,
So that there is something perdurable for us in the dark,
    A word like a stream, like sleepless lovers,
And a goblet full of wine and intrepid thirst for life,
    And sacred memory, too, to keep us wakeful at night.

3

In vain we think we can hide our hearts in our chests,
    In vain we sequester our daring—for who would
Stand in our way and forbid us to know the heights of joy?
    A godly fire burns by day and by night to break out
And liberate us. So come with me—the open calls to us,
    Promising what is uniquely ours, far though we may have to go.
One thing is sure: whether in the middle of the day
    Or at midnight, that which is given to all waits for us,
Though there is also that which belongs to each one of us only,
    And in our comings and goings we reach the horizon we can.
Jubilant madness will turn mockery against the mocking
    When, in the holiness of night, it possesses the poets—
So let's go to the isthmus where the open sea roars
    By Parnassus and the snow shines on the Delphic rocks,
The land of the Olympians, to the heights of Cithaeron,
    By the pines and the vineyards rich with grapes,
The land of Thebes, the land of Ismenos, and Cadmus—
    From there he came—he leads us back—the god to come.

4

Blessed Greece! You, home of all the heavenly ones—
    Is it so, that which we once heard in our youth?
Festal hall whose floor is the sea, whose tables are mountains,
    Truly built for one cause by the ancients.
But where are the thrones? And the temples? And the vessels
    Filled with nectar? And the songs to please the gods?
And where are the shining oracles, claiming distances still?
    Delphi sleeps—where is the great music of Fate?
Where is the fast one? Where does it dawn on us,
    Out of a serene air, thundering, ubiquitous joy?
Father! the chant that went from one mouth to another
    A thousand times: none of them lived life alone.
Freely given, such goodness brings happiness; shared with strangers,
    It brings joy; the word grows in power as it sleeps.
Father, serene one! The ancient sign we are heirs to
    Echoes as far as it can—piercing, creating.
So the heavenly ones arrive, and with a shudder
    Their day reaches its fullness, out of the shadows, among men.

5

At first they go almost unseen as they appear, children rush
    To meet them—the excitement is too bright, too blinding—
So that the people shy away from them, and a demigod hardly knows
    By what name to call those who bring him gifts.
But their courage is striking. Their joy fills his heart
    And he hardly knows what to do with the goodness they bring.
He makes, he broods; the ordinary almost becomes holy to him,
    Touched by the blessing of his foolish, gentle hand.
The heavenly ones tolerate this for as long as they can,
    Then in true passion they themselves descend, and humankind
Grows close to happiness and daylight and to really seeing the visible—
    The apparitions of those who long ago were called One and All
Filling deeply the hearts of those who had given up on expression,
    And consummating every longing, first and alone.
It must be human nature—when goodness is there before him,
    As a god has made it to be, he doesn't see it or know it,
He feels he must suffer for his gift. Now, however,
    He calls it his most beloved in words that blossom like flowers.

6

Now it is his intention to honor the blessed gods in earnest.
    Sincerely and truly may all share in the act of praise.
Nothing that is unfit for the holy ones should see the light of day.
    Half-heartedness, mere presence, is nothing to them.
So that they can be worthy to stand before the gods
    The masses create a dream of order amongst themselves
And from this they build beautiful temples and cities
    That preside like enduring nobility over the shores—
But where are they? Where are the flourishing festal sites?
    Thebes and Athens have faded. The din of weapons
Has fallen silent in Olympia. The golden chariots of war games
    Are gone. And the ships of Corinth go undecorated now.
Why have they fallen silent, the ancient, holy theaters?
    Why is there no joyous dancing among the sacred rites?
Once a god could mark a man as chosen—why not now?
    To be marked by a god once was to be transformed;
Or the god appeared himself in human form and as a comfort
    To those rejoicing brought an indelible end to his feast.

7

But, friend—we come too late. Yes, the gods are alive,
    But far beyond us, over our heads—in another world.
Their existence is endless, and they seem to care very little
    If we survive—they offer us this indifference as salvation.
For a weak vessel cannot always be a fit home for them;
    Only rarely can humanity bear the full presence of divinity,
And so to dream is to know them best. Wandering helps us,
    Like sleep, and our need and the night make us stronger,
Until the heroes have grown enough in the cradle
    And hearts grow strong as they had been, like those in the heavens.
They come in thunder. And so now sleep seems
    Better to me than to be so bereft of holy companionship
And to wait in dark hope and to be so uncertain of what to do
    Or to say—I don't know—what of poets in a dark time?
You tell me they are like holy priests of the wine god,
    Who travel from land to land in the sanctity of night.

8

And once in the past—to us it seems long ago, indeed—
    All those who had made our lives joyous ascended
And the Father turned his face away from humankind
    And grief was felt earnestly on this earth,
Until, at last, a quiet spirit, the genius, appeared, bringing us
    Heavenly comfort, he who proclaimed the end of days
And then disappeared, leaving, as a sign that he had been here
    And would come again, the gifts of a heavenly choir,
That humankind may find themselves in rejoicing,
    For joy in the spirit of greatness had grown for too long
Among us and even now there is a dearth of the strength
    That can bear the limits of joy—so quietly our thanks live on.
Bread is the fruit of the earth, blessed by the light of day,
    And from the god of thunder we are given the joy of wine.
So these turn our thoughts to the spirits of the heavens
    Who once were here and will return again in time,
And so the poets sing earnestly of the wine god
    And offer their praise to the ancient—something true.

9

Yes—they are right to say he reconciles day and night
    And leads the stars of the heavens to rise and set,
Always joyful, like the evergreen branches of the spruce,
    Which he loves, and the ivy garland he has chosen
Because it survives—it preserves traces of the departed gods
    For the godless ones, those left in darkness.
What the ancient song foretold of the children of God—
    Look! It is fulfilled—the fruit of Hesperia.
Wondrous—just as he foretold, he is ours;
    It is right for us to have faith—but so much resists;
There is a fault in us; we are as unmoved as shadows until
    Father Ether is known as ours to one and all.
But in our time the exalted son comes, reaching us from Syria,
    Amongst the shadows brandishing his torch.
The blessed wise ones perceive; laughter is born in the hearts
    Of prisoners, and their eyes thaw to the light.
Titans sleep and dream gently in the arms of the earth,
    And even the hound of jealousy, Cerberus—he drinks and sleeps.

Interdependence and Paranoia

Three point seven million years ago, just before
a massive volcanic eruption, two adults and a child
of the species *Australopithecus* walked on soft earth together.
They are the first creatures we know who walked
with the foot of a human, with a big toe, a hallux,
that aligns with the other toes, that is not opposable.
Two adults and a child—the child's footprints are
more plentiful—smaller steps—and are very close
to the adults, whose footprints overlap each other.
A picture of trust and care, guarded jealously by the earth.

Paranoia is the shadow of care because at the extreme you accuse
yourself—I accuse myself—of disloyalty:
to the church, to the left, to the Jews.
But I mostly know I am a good person;
what I want is to be free to use my intellect,
and to encourage others to do so as well—
to favor the rigorous intellect and yet belong—
paranoia, self-doubt, self-accusation,
like the overlapping steps of the adults, double, impure—

and trust and care like the pure prints of the child,
staying close, having learned, not independent,
but interdependent—she knows she must walk forward
because the elders will not leave her behind.

Beginner's Mind

—for Countée Cullen

1

There are thirty-one
ways of seeing.

If you trust me,
you are complete.

2

Adorno on jazz—
as my teacher might say:

what a strange expression,
deal-breaker.

Thelonious Monk's America—
who has forgotten

as long as this?

3

What an idiot,
Ward Churchill—

what a dumb thing he said,
comparing bankers to Eichmann.

What bankers do
to people,

people do to people.

4

Pointing the finger.
Walking the dog.

Not minding the rain.

5

I used to love that poem,
"Heritage,"

by Countée Cullen.
You can tell he really

doesn't know what it means
to be Black,—

I really got that part.

6

Phillis Wheatley
treated poetry

like a game,
the child-genius.

White people know nothing,
Black people know

nothing's nothing.

7

Her name was
Lorraine Embry.

I always knew there wasn't
though I expected love.

8

Before
you were a beginner,

you were someone.
Flesh and blood,

your biographer says.
We were, then, you and I,

strong as ice.

9

Incident—
more shameful

than menstruation
to the other.

So there you said
the word

we can't understand.

10

You were Phi Beta Kappa too:
teachers want blood,

blown-blood
back in the body.

11

I won't read your novel—
I am just not

into dissociation.
If that's all

you know about me,
that's enough—

orange moon.

12

Beginners understand greatness.
Only adults

think it has to do
with death . . .

that's boring—
Greatness has to do

with love.

13

But what if
I say something

crazy—
that you're great

in a Harlem window,
the closet

of imagination.

14

Rumors—
critical thinking

about to begin,
forever.

15

Something must be said
for sadness—

on the couch
with my son,

memory
of that sadness

is joy.

Reading Through • (The Catalog of the Getty in the Pandemic Era)

1

Can you think of something more pretentious
than translating poetry from a language
you can't understand?

Well, probably so—

I love my teacher, the archetype of the spiritual guide,
but he too has some of the foolishness he spots
contemptuously in his colleagues.

He translated Japanese and Polish poetry he couldn't read
into his own idiom of English
and both books became available at Barnes and Noble:

cis-het white male boomer privilege incarnate.
Simple, plain, easy—we love them too.

2

Reading the collected poetry
of Nikki Giovanni—

it starts in the mid-sixties;
there is some real antisemitic shit there.

Everyone is a radical—
the point is to find out what root

is yours,
what soil is ready for you.

3

The debate can go on forever:

if everybody is something,
then nobody is really that something.

Well, I have news for you—
that's how language works.

Words don't mean anything sometimes.
The scene of characters in your voice

disappears into the surrounding darkness,
and the audience

doesn't get their money's worth,
petals scattered at sea.

4

My wife—
she is probably who this poem
is really about,

but I don't want to write about her,
so I won't.

She's a woman of color
who can pass.

I learned so much from her—
about her,

about love.

And now that we have
nothing left
to teach each other,

I can ask my art
how the story ends.

5

It ends the way most stories end,
in loneliness—

at least the Mossad stops harassing you
when you're dead.

Notice I didn't say all stories end in loneliness—
what about movies, readings, etc.?

Mimesis—

we've all survived an apocalypse,
being born.

Poetry is as lonely as birth
for some of us—

living silence.

6

Figures are black in the pottery of ancient Greece
because they are men.

That was the convention for centuries.
Women were white.

How can the black man be for the white man
and not be his dick?—
the question asked recently by Douglas Kearney.

Look at what white men
have done to black boys—

the reality of the nightmare in the mirror,
the urn of quietness.

Tension, ambiguity, irony, indeterminacy—
up from the south:

singing body,
whispering flame.

7

At the Getty there is a bust in black stone
of an African man
from the eighteenth century.

It shows his hewn pectoral muscles
and his nipples—

very realistic, life-like,
those nipples of the eighteenth century.

Realism in sculpture
has progressed very little since then—

film, photography—
so easy to say in a poem, *I refute it thus*—

the impossible half
of the realist's desire.

8

Looking at Goya's *Bullfight*,
a small image of it next to a box of text,
I peer closely

looking for dark-skinned people.

My skin is
not dark enough for me to know

how dark is dark enough.

There are Spaniards in the picture;
room for doubt.

Divorce is the sign of knowledge in our time—
Williams said that.

Dark woman,
he said too.

It's not all about skin—
hair, eyes, features—

racism makes me the reader
of a language

I don't wholly hope to understand.

Abgrund

The bell—
it rings in the morning,
everywhere.

Meditations • (On the Albums of Julieta Venegas)

2 - Bueninvento, "Casa Abandonada"

Trots them.
The thick house, the nobody gives house
on Buffalone.
Red brick stick, drip trap
saint Joe's—
everybody says nobody and almost nobody comes.

To remember remembering as this—
same game, some gum
the riverview golf courts for sunnytime tennis hits.
Them running far,
far-run, far-flung, flag hung so high
on Buffalone.

Like the wings of Buffalone,
a post-bus girl lost labor's union's joints—
they got moore, moor—
so good trots them.
Ceiling fan, fan of the finger, the wafer-thin,
have to think it over risen again.

9 - *La Enamorada*, "Mis Muertos"

The fair way, fare thee well, will you wonder
at the ghost,
the pacemaker-stent?
Here we go again, there you have it—they can't move
a cat's ninth muscle.

We dangle
her pronoun like a fire-fangled gown,
the grandma-ghost.

Here's the thing,
there's the catch.
He's dangling from the line, he swallowed the hook.
Time is a train.
From any given point the willow marshes on.

1 - *Aquí,* "Oportunidad"

Accordihum.
The beginning and the hemmed.
The noise of childhood, the sound of a crying voice
may not be your home.
All the nos of childhood,—
build your home on the glacier of no.

You cannot separate your beauty from money.
Money is like snow.
Heartmelt in the accordion music-show.
Build your home on the glacier of no.

One Echo

"If the British were to leave India, who would then be the rulers? Is it possible that two nations, the Muslim and Hindu, could sit on the same throne and remain in power? To hope that both would remain equal is to desire the impossible and the inconceivable."

—Sir Syed Ahmed Khan, 1883

Mind-way

1

The source of wisdom in you
cannot be exhausted by your limbs

nor by the tongue in your mouth.

If you seek to exhaust it,
loss will resound like laughter,

laughter only you understand.

If you trust yourself, truly,
you may be remembered for many generations—

the source of wisdom in you
is laughter at laughter,

autumn, a young gardener at dusk.

2

Anger
is like honey.

It keeps forever;
it rewards you.

Mind-way accepts anger,

it does not ask it to be
the uroboros,—

we breathe with two lungs,
one mouth,

two nostrils,
one body.

3

Origins:
redwoods in memory,

their loneliness
among so many of their kind.

What is your question
for life?

So many choose
to leave the universe
as they found it—

I believe it is their choice,—
to listen.

4

The experience of giving up—
white shirt,

white flag.

The song of experience
is like a zombie's cataract.

Lay it to rest,
the sack of this word.

Children will learn on instruments
yet unmade.

The dance of madness
is like a distant wind—

to experience
the intimate freedom of infinite space.

5

Mirror in mirror:
Spiegel im Spiegel—

to live without teleology,
if you are able—

inner destiny.

It's different,
they assured me,
the survivors.

Neither better nor worse.

The sky in a coffin,
the ethical sunflower,—

laughter at laughter,
a young gardener at dusk.

6

On principle—
the sewn seams you loved

in your childhood blanket,
opal, microtextured,

the smallest sensory pleasures
at the soft tips

of your fingers,
ridges and edges—

keep your love of principles
close to you.

7

Young man,
they wanted you to be the best

so they could come for you

with their imagination
like a syndicate.

It takes others
to make one the best.

What age wants from youth,
a fibrous fire.

Don't be afraid to be the best—

slender reed,
that bit, ever better.

On Loving Narcissus

The little ice ages,
centuries of frozen streams under bridges,
and with summer's cool touch

the impossible forgetting:

he was so beautiful
I lost myself
with desire
that would never come again.

It was unconsummated,
my passion—

how can the gods make one
so fair

and then turn
to the little ice ages,
their crystalline blades of anger,

so the imagination gives up
on the tresses
it was braiding for love

and swallows its tongue?

Critical Portrait

1

Depressive realism—
in his work on cosmology Michio Kaku states his conviction
that the fate of our universe
will be an ending of nearly absolute cold
as it expands—
the fate of heat death—
and that the only hope for life is to find a portal to another universe.

This is the message of science—
how can any scientist not be shaken by this?

As for the science of writing:
let's focus on five paragraphs and pentameter lines
and the Oxford comma
for as long as we can,
and then, when we must, let's face the question of why
we still know
we can write something meaningful
in the screen-light or firelight of Kaku's sentence.

2

The victory of negation—
nothing lasts forever; there is no forever—

the reality of death is very sad but, in a way, ordinary,
I have seen it—

it is the idea of death,
of returning to nothingness, that is unsettling to me.

Fundamentalists have their beginning and their end—
can one be
a fundamentalist of science?

The science of writing:
what began with the idea to tally debt in clay,
with imaginatively seen cracks on a tortoise shell—

where does it end?
My teacher said with a guarded laugh
that there is no end to the path of a scholar—

funny I was taught to write just that at the first limit of my stories,
not an end—

just the end.

3

Jedes Seiende ist ein Ereignis:
Every being is an event.

I learned this as a teacher from another teacher,
having been abandoned by God in Germany—

does it follow from modernism's darkness,
the lesson of loving kindness?

Today on my walk
I saw the back of a handyman's pickup truck,
filled with his tools—

no leaves in there,
I suppose he uses them all often—

or he is not from this part of the world,
where in late November the sycamores descend in daylight—

4

Writing is a science.
It's just that some sciences are more difficult than others.

Mathematicians invented the zero.
It falls to writers to solve the problem of zero.

The indigenous people of California used fire
to clear the ground for the plants that would nourish their prey.

The fire of zero—
let us see if we can begin to rewrite this sentence.

Subject and a verb:
The indigenous people of California used fire.

Have used, had used,
were using:

there are only a handful of ways to write history.

5

The innocence of science—
like the innocence of Whittier in *Snow-Bound*,
his real work long done,
waiting hopefully to be recognized for what he has made.

How can writing help us
to find a way out of this universe to another,
to survive?

Whittier begins with the memory of clearing a path as a child
to his barn
on the morning after a blizzard,

and America loved it,
an innocent memory from long before the Civil War:

it falls to poets to tell the history
that the science of history cannot save—

here,
in the world of the ubiquitous camera-phone,

to try to solve the problem of the future
when the perpetual present will cease to be,

and the love that moves the sun and the other stars
becomes the shrieking of the mindless wind.

Genius and Milosz

In the twentieth century,
I met my teacher's teacher,
a great poet, Czeslaw Milosz.

He believed every poet should
write of their experience with clarity—
otherwise nothingness would win too soon.

Dissociation, fragmentation, deliberate irrationality:
just so much turbidity in the human race's necessary waters.

The idea of genius of a genius:
every place and generation
need their idea of the ultimate possible
to protect themselves from a mad form of hope.

So why do I want to think all of my students are geniuses?

Perhaps a useful distinction
is the experience of genius
and the identity of genius.

All of us
can experience an awakening of a new sense of the possible,
but that mostly happens
in the private chamber of relationships
that leave our identity unchanged.
So what else do I want for my students,
if not to help them find the expression of their genius?

Experiences that will nourish their senses of
freedom, happiness, gratitude—

the accomplishment
that an old Milosz
said to me at his apartment door as I left,
stunned and shaped by my afternoon with greatness:

dobje,—
it is well between us.

Mission San Juan Capistrano

—for Carolyn Porter

1

Solstice light came at me like a memory
As I walked out through the chapel doors
Away from the darkness of its gold

Into the midmorning rich and silent air.
There were no schoolchildren touring there
But the problem still lay heavy on me

And I sat on the bench to observe the fountain
Where the ghost of water played and splashed
And I spoke like a man possessed

My question for those who love to know:
How could your God have let these warrior-priests
Bring their diseases to the children

Who called out to their mothers here?
I read this autumn the best answer of any yet:
God doesn't want us to know why,

For then we would give up on justice forever.
But the death and suffering here of these innocents
Eats like frostbite at my mind.

Like the fire of lighting from a strike so dark
It goes unseen, the friar in a simple cassock
Was seated next to me out of nowhere, and replied at once:

Your idea of innocence is too easy to mistake
For grace, pilgrim-child.
We are all fallen—we all must be saved.

Don't trouble yourself with questions that suggest
You know more than the Almighty.
The chapel is the weapon against the wretchedness of man.

I turned to test his eyes for wisdom, but he was gone,
And then the memory came in earnest,
Walking those grounds with my two young children

Half a decade before, taking pictures, reading graves,
Picking up books in the gift store and putting them away.
And riding back home from the mission on the train—

Traveling backwards in our seats, seeing where we'd been
A second before, like the angel of history
Traveling home, his maps taken from him by the wind.

2

I returned that evening in my dreams,
To the graveyard—two thousand unmarked graves
Celebrated by a crucifix, the talon-X:

One by one, or in pairs, the other tourists left
And I was standing in the shadow of the wall
Where I heard him call me from the Father's grave—

Don't be troubled, he said, *Come here.*
You are like an old man who has forgotten
The words of the hymn and yet begins to sing.

I knew he knew me by some dark magic
And I feared what he knew of me
Was just the final truth, so thoroughly had he

Been possessed by his God. My heart felt heavy
But my conscience stirred me to speak:
What did you save? Their bodies are all left here

Who came as you bid them, fascinated or afraid.
And their souls—who knows where the soul is
Or where it goes—it is their bodies that you murdered

In the name of an ever-loving God
That you are left with. The will is nothing.
There is nothing to save but the body,

And there you failed like Milton's Lucifer.
He began to laugh and walked away.
There was no tolling bell from the Mission church,

And I woke at midmorning with the shadow
Of the unsaved across my spirit,
Wondering where he had gone to out of my dream.

3

Then there was a gardener no one else could see
Clipping at the roses in the courtyard
And as he brushed the flowers bending to the ground

The yellow petals fell upon his darkened shoes.
He looked up at me after I had watched him for a while
And I recognized again the ghost

Of Father Serra. *Still searching,* he said,
In the garden for what is found in time
At the altar of the heart.

I said: *I know I am haunted.*
The death of the innocent happened first to me,
I was taken from my mother

Because I was deathly ill—
They saved me in the hospital,
But the part of the spirit that reposes

In the knowledge God is good—
I was too wounded by the loss of comfort
In my torment to feel His presence anymore.

He cut and handed me a yellow rose
And placed his hand upon my shoulder,
Reaching up slightly and squinting at the sun.

So you have your poems. The temporality of God
Is like the temporality of the poem.
So much suffering and happiness and labor

Goes into the series that you write,
And they create one presence that is as if
It happened in the daylight all at once.

So it is with God. You are His poem.
He is writing you. I thanked him and wandered
In the courtyard and sat on a bench a while

Before I took out my notebook and began to write,
A poem to the innocents lost by the diseases
Of the servants of my family's God:

I will never forget you, I wrote,
And I ask that you do not give up on me.
Our innocence could topple stones

At the final wakefulness,
When we will see the judgment on their coming here
Cast down from history's empty throne.

4

Months later I was there again
And there was no ghost of Serra but a class
Of schoolchildren led from one room to the next

By a serene guide and their teacher
Who wore a necklace of a crucifix in gold.
I wanted so to follow them,

For in truth I had nothing better to do
And there was one boy at the back of the group
Who was taking pictures with his phone

And I wished I could breach the walls of separateness
And ask him what he was looking for
In what he photographed, precocious spirit.

And as the children walked away
Following the voices of the teacher and the guide
He turned and took a photograph of me,

Or what was behind me,
I cannot be sure—
I only know that he and I were together there.

Songs of Solitude

Love

You will have been wrong
before and after.

If you give up now
you can harvest the emptiness of candlelight.

You looked so long at the outsider,
his cold breath on the window.

Faith

He, my father, held on to his belief in his own goodness
like a tree to the sky.

For Melanie

Spousal—
I somehow found this earth,—
the light half, too

About the Author

Brian Glaser was born in Detroit, Michigan, the eldest of two children of Jack Glaser, a theologian, and Mary Ellen Glaser, an educator and social worker. He was educated at the University of California, Berkeley. In 2003, he married dancer and choreographer Melanie Ríos, with whom he has two children, Andoe and John. In 2005, he joined the faculty at Chapman University, where he currently teaches in the department of English. His previous poetry collections, *All the Hills* and *Contradictions*, were published by Shanti Arts (2019, 2020).

SHANTI ARTS

NATURE ▪ ART ▪ SPIRIT

Please visit us online
to browse our entire book catalog,
including poetry collections and fiction,
books on travel, nature, healing, art,
photography, and more.

Also take a look at our highly regarded art
and literary journal, *Still Point Arts Quarterly*,
which may be downloaded for free.

www.shantiarts.com

CPSIA information can be obtained
at www.ICGtesting.com
Printed in the USA
FSHW011755171221
87016FS